Goodnight, Nisha

by Amelia Shanks

illustrated by Janice Bowles

EDUCATORS PUBLISHING SERVICE
Cambridge and Toronto

Series Authors: Kay Kovalevs and Alison Dewsbury
Series Consultant: Melinda Rice
Commissioning Editors: Sarah Russell, Bonnie Lass, and Sethany Rancier Alongi
Senior Editorial Manager: Sheila Neylon
Text by Amelia Shanks
Illustrated by Janice Bowles
Edited by Katherine Steward and Laura A. Woollett
Designed by Kathryn de Reus and Maria Vallianos

Making Connections® program developed by Educators Publishing Service,
a division of School Specialty Publishing and by Harcourt Education, a division of
Reed International Books Australia Pty Ltd.

ISBN 0-8388-3313-6
ISBN 978-0-8388-3313-1

2010 2009 2008 2007 2006
10 9 8 7 6 5 4 3 2 1

Printed in China

"Goodnight, Nisha," said Mom.
"Goodnight, Mom," said Nisha.
Mom turned off the light.

Every night was the same,
thought Nisha. Mom said
goodnight. She turned off
the light.

Mom checked on Ravi, Nisha's little brother. Then she read while Nisha's dad watched TV.

In the dark, Nisha had
a thought. What if Ravi isn't
in bed?

What if Mom isn't reading?
And what if Dad isn't watching
TV?

Maybe Ravi's juggling five
colored balls, thought Nisha.

Ravi's a famous clown. He's
wearing a clown suit and a big
red nose. Juggling five balls is
hard, but Ravi is good at it.

Maybe Mom's walking on the high wire, thought Nisha.

Mom's a famous acrobat.
She's wearing a white costume.
The wire is high up, but Mom's
very brave.

Maybe Dad's taming a lion,
thought Nisha.

Dad's a famous lion tamer.
He's wearing a black suit and
long boots. The lion is large and
loud, but Dad's not scared.

Nisha sat up in bed. Maybe
I should just see what they're
doing, she thought. She opened
the door and tiptoed down
the hall.

Ravi was in bed. Nisha looked
in the living room. Mom was
reading while Dad watched TV.

Nisha tiptoed back to her
room. She got into bed. In the
dark, she had a thought. What
if Grandma . . .